Who Works Here?

Zoo

by Lola M. Schaefer

Heinemann Library
Chicago, Illinois

Designed by Wilkinson Design
Printed in Hong Kong

05 04 03 02 01
10 9 8 7 6 5 4 3 2 1

Library of Congress Cataloging-in-Publication Data
Schaefer, Lola M., 1950-
    Zoo / by Lola M. Schaefer.
        p. cm. -- (Who works here?)
    Includes bibliographical references (p.).
    ISBN 1-58810-128-2 (library binding)
    1. Zoos--Employees--Juvenile literature. [1. Zoos--Employees. 2. Occupations.] I. Title.

QL76 .S29 2001
590'.7'3--dc21

                                                        00-058095

Acknowledgments
Photography by Phil Martin and Zoo Atlanta.
Special thanks to all the staff at Zoo Atlanta, and to workers everywhere who take pride in what they do.

Every effort has been made to contact copyright holders of any material reproduced in this book. Any omissions will be rectified in subsequent printings if notice is given to the publisher.

Some words are shown in bold, **like this.**
You can find out what they mean by looking in the glossary.

Contents

What Is a Zoo?

People visit zoos all over the United States to learn about animals from around the world.

A zoo is a place where a trained **staff** cares for animals. Everyone works together to keep the animals healthy and comfortable. The zoo is open to the public. Visitors often pay a **fee** to enter the zoo and learn more about the animals.

At the zoo, animals live in **habitats.** These habitats have the same kinds of trees, bushes, and flowers that grow in the animals' natural homes. The staff feeds the animals the same kinds of food they would eat in the wild. A zoo is a safe place to see different kinds of animals.

This zoo is in Atlanta, Georgia. The map shows where the people in this book work. Many zoos in the United States look like this.

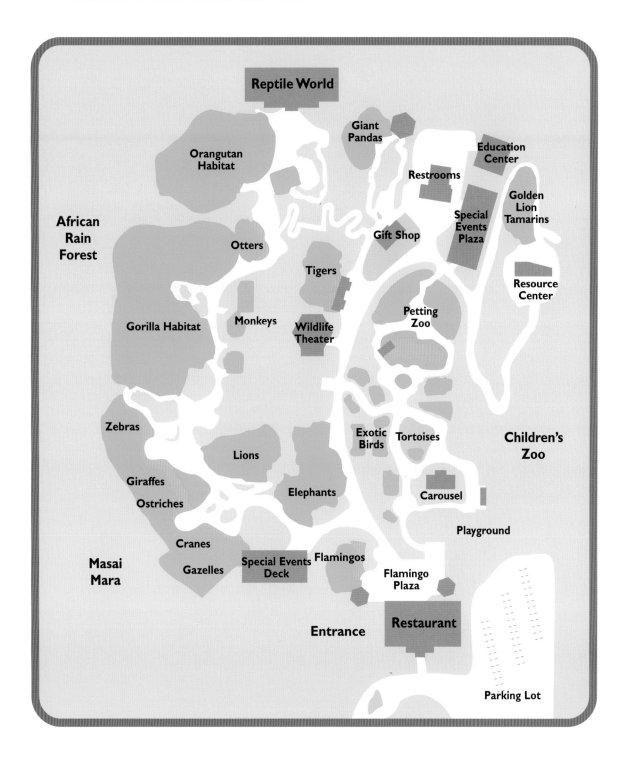

Animal Keeper

Sprina is an animal keeper. The giraffes hear her voice and come to eat apples and carrots.

An animal keeper cares for animals at the zoo. This person serves meals, cleans the **habitats,** and trains the animals to accept **medical** care. Every day, the keeper observes the animals closely and notes any changes in **behavior** or health.

Sprina, like most animal keepers, has a college **degree** in science. Many keepers continue to learn and earn another degree in an area of animal science, like **zoology.** This training helps keepers understand the needs of animals.

This animal keeper is loading hay into the wheelbarrow to carry into the giraffe barn.

Zoo Veterinarian

A zoo veterinarian is responsible for the health of the animals at the zoo. This person gives each animal a yearly check-up. When animals become sick or injured, the veterinarian gives them medicine or performs **surgery** to help them heal.

Dr. Maria is a zoo veterinarian. She is using a **microscope** to study the blood of a sick gorilla.

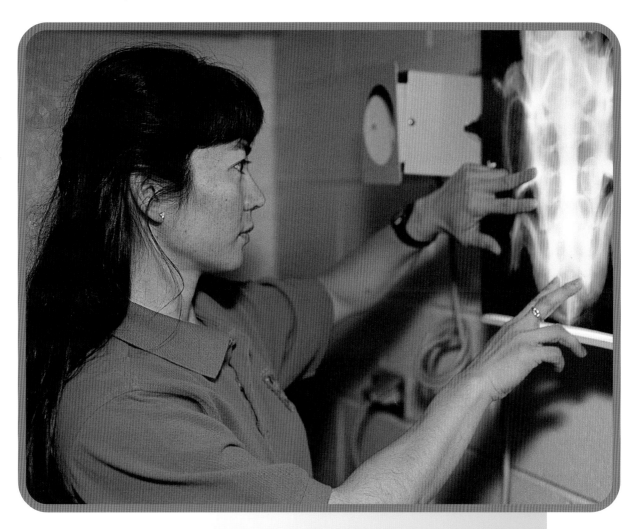

Dr. Maria studies an **x-ray** of a turtle with eggs to learn why the turtle cannot lay her eggs.

Zoo veterinarians need special training. First they receive a college **degree,** then they attend veterinarian school for another four years. Afterward, they work with animals in **clinics** or zoos for 4-6 years before becoming a veterinarian. They need to know how to care for many different kinds of animals.

Commissary Manager

A zoo commissary manager prepares the meals for the animals. He or she orders the food. The commissary manager checks that the food is fresh, safe, and filled with the **nutrients** the animals need to stay healthy.

Gloria is the commissary manager at this zoo. She is measuring the fruit and vegetables for the lemurs.

Zoo commissary managers chop and mix meats, fruits, and vegetables for the different animals. Then, they store the food in refrigerators before it is delivered to the keepers. To become a commissary manager, people go to college for about six years to learn about animals and what foods they need to be fed.

Here, Gloria divides the mice that will be used as live food for the reptiles.

Senior Research Associate

Rebecca is a senior research associate at a zoo. She is recording how often these giant pandas eat.

The purpose of a scientific study in a zoo is to learn how to protect an animal in the wild. Senior research associates study animals to collect **data** to help save animals and their **habitats** around the world. Each study begins with a question about an animal.

Rebecca uses data in her computer to find answers to her questions about animals.

A senior research associate watches an animal in its **habitat** to learn how it eats, sleeps, and plays. This data will help answer the study's question. Rebecca, like other senior research associates, has college **degrees** in science and animal **behavior.**

Lead Keeper

A lead keeper is responsible for the care of one group of animals at the zoo. He or she makes the daily schedule of jobs for that **staff**. Together, the lead keeper and staff feed, clean, and record the health of the animals.

Laura is the lead keeper of the orangutans.

Lead keepers must know a lot about animals. Some lead keepers have studied animal science in college. Others have worked with animals on farms, in **clinics,** or at zoos. And, some lead keepers have studied animals in college and worked with animals for many years.

Here, Laura is working in the orangutan **habitat,** watching to make sure they are healthy.

Assistant Curator of Horticulture

The assistant curator of **horticulture** plants and cares for all the live flowers, shrubs, and trees at the zoo. This person usually wears strong boots, gloves, and safety glasses. When using loud machines, he or she also wears earplugs for ear protection.

Ed, an assistant curator of horticulture, plants shrubs on one side of a hornbill **habitat.**

Ed prunes a young tree along one of
the visitor paths at the zoo.

Many assistant curators of horticulture have a
college **degree.** They learn more skills each year at
conferences. Part of their training explains the use of
safe, non-poisonous plants near animals and people.

Security Supervisor

The security supervisor keeps the zoo safe for the animals, zoo **staff,** and visitors. He or she uses a radio to stay in contact with the other security officers at the zoo at all times. The security staff helps people understand and obey the safety rules of the zoo, such as keeping hands and feet outside the **habitats.**

Doug, the security supervisor, walks with a zoo **employee** as she carries a cash bag to the gift shop.

Security supervisors receive advanced security training. They learn about laws and how to enforce them correctly. They know **first aid** and how to help people with health problems. When a new animal arrives at the zoo, the security staff learns the animal's **behavior** and makes plans to keep the animal and visitors safe.

The security supervisor gives a boy directions to the gorillas.

Education Programs Manager

An education programs manager plans and gives **workshops,** tours, and zoo mobile visits for school groups and families. This person and the education **staff** put together loan boxes that contain videos, **biofacts,** books, and activities on animals and their **habitats.**

This education programs manager shows a group of teachers the materials they can borrow from the zoo.

Angela, an education programs manager, makes giant panda bingo cards for classroom teachers.

Education programs managers have a college **degree** in science or education. Many continue at college for another degree. They enjoy showing the zoo services to people of all ages.

Education Programs Assistant

Daniel is an education programs assistant. He is showing a girl that reptiles are covered in dry **scales.**

An education programs assistant teaches children and adults how to protect the different animals of the world. This educator uses live animals and **biofacts** to explain the place each animal has in the balance of nature.

Daniel, like other education program assistants, trained for one month at the zoo. He learned how to present important information to the public. Daniel likes his job because he helps people know why the different animals are important.

Education programs assistants move small, cold-blooded animals in coolers to protect them from cold and hot temperatures.

Distance Learning Instructor

Distance learning connects **rural** areas with the zoo and its education programs. Using a **studio,** a distance learning instructor works with school children many miles away. Cameras and **microphones** in the studio send the instructor's face and voice into the classrooms.

Megan is a distance learning instructor. She is welcoming three different classrooms to a lesson on giant pandas.

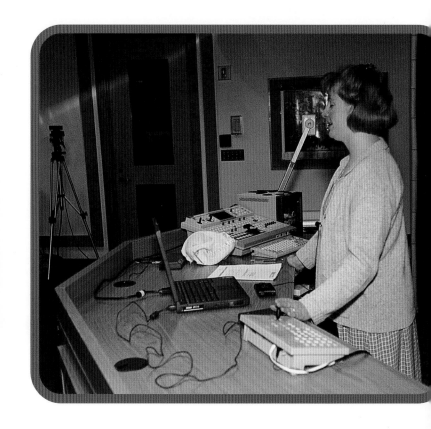

Using these TV screens, the instructor can see the school children and the program at the same time.

School children view the distance learning instructor on **monitors** in their classrooms. Using microphones, the children can ask questions of the instructor and zoo experts during the program. This kind of distance learning helps children go on a behind-the-scenes field trip of the zoo.

The Business of the Zoo

Lisa is an assistant public relations coordinator. She is giving an **interview** to a children's book author and photographer.

Assistant Public Relations Coordinator

An assistant public relations coordinator takes newspaper, magazine, and TV people through the zoo. This person informs the public about any new events or changes at the zoo. The assistant public relations coordinator **communicates** with many people every day.

Accounting Manager

An accounting manager is responsible for all the money the zoo makes and spends. This person makes sure that the bills and the **employees** are paid on time. The accounting manager also puts the money the zoo makes into the bank.

Cheryl, an accounting manager, is adding all the entrance gate **receipts** for one day.

27

Deputy Zoo Director

Steve is the deputy director of a zoo. He is speaking with another staff member about a new gate at the entrance to the zoo.

A deputy zoo director works with the different **department** managers. Together they try to make the zoo friendly for visitors. A deputy zoo director provides materials, like lumber, lights, tools, and machines, to the **staff** so they can do a good job.

Steve, like most deputy zoo directors, has a regular college **degree,** and another degree in a special area. Deputy zoo directors have usually worked in many other jobs at the zoo. This helps them understand what the different **employees** need.

Here, Steve is speaking with a builder about a new **habitat** for red pandas.

Glossary

behavior how an animal or person eats, sleeps, works, and plays with others

biofact natural object from a living thing, like a snake skin, elephant tusk, or shark tooth

clinic room or building where people or animals can receive medical treatment

communicate to share information, ideas, or feelings with another person by talking, writing, or drawing

conference meeting of people in which ideas and information are shared

data information or facts

degree rank that a college gives a student who has finished his or her studies

department part of a zoo, store, or other business that has a particular purpose

employee person who works for someone else and is paid to do so

fee money that is paid to get into something; money that is paid for a service

first aid help given to a sick or injured person while waiting for regular medical help

habitat place in which an animal or plant lives

horticulture the growing of fruits, vegetables, flowers, and other plants

interview meeting at which someone is asked questions

medical to do with doctors or medicine

microphone instrument that picks up sound waves so they can be broadcast, recorded, or made louder

microscope instrument used to make tiny things look larger

monitor visual display screen; like the screen on a computer

nutrient proteins, vitamins, and minerals needed by animals, humans, and plants to stay healthy and strong

receipt piece of paper showing that money has been paid

rural to do with the countryside

scales thin, flat, hard plates that cover and protect some fish and reptiles

staff group of people who work for a company or person

studio place where movies, television, and radio shows are made or recorded

surgery medical treatment that involves repairing, removing, or replacing injured or diseased parts of the body

workshop short educational program for a small group of people that talks about skills they use and need for their jobs

x-ray invisible ray that can go through solid things; used to study the bones and organs inside the body

zoology the scientific study of animals

More Books to Read

Deedrick, Tami. *Zoo Keepers.* Minnetonka, Minn.: Capstone Press, Inc., 1998.

Kallen, Stuart A. *The Zoo.* Edina, Minn.: ABDO Publishing Company, 1997.

Moses, Amy. *At the Zoo.* Chanhassen, Minn.: The Child's World, Inc., 1997.

Schomp, Virginia. *If You Were a Zookeeper.* Tarrytown, N.Y.: Marshall Cavendish Corporation, 1999.

Index